FROGS

Life Cycles

ABDO
Publishing Company

A Buddy Book
by Julie Murray

VISIT US AT
www.abdopublishing.com

Published by ABDO Publishing Company, 4940 Viking Drive, Edina, Minnesota 55435.

Printed in the United States.

Coordinating Series Editor: Sarah Tieck
Contributing Editor: Michael P. Goecke
Graphic Design: Deb Coldiron
Cover Photograph: Photos.com
Interior Photographs/Illustrations: Animals Animals - Earth Scenes: Scott W. Smith (pages 17, 21), Media Bakery, Minden Pictures, Photos.com

Library of Congress Cataloging-in-Publication Data

Murray, Julie, 1969–
    Frogs / Julie Murray.
        p. cm. — (Life cycles)
    Includes index.
    ISBN-13: 978-1-59928-707-2
    ISBN-10: 1-59928-707-2
        1. Frogs—Life cycles—Juvenile literature. I. Title.

QL668.E2M864 2007
597.8'9—dc22

                                        2006034264

Table Of Contents

What Is A Life Cycle?

Frogs are living things. The world is made up of many kinds of life. People are alive. So are eagles, crickets, snakes, and pine trees.

The first frogs lived more than 100 million years ago.

Every living thing has a life cycle. A life cycle is made up of many changes and processes. During a life cycle, living things are born, they grow, and they reproduce. And eventually, they die. Different living things start life and grow up in unique ways.

What do you know about the life cycle of frogs?

Meet The Frog

There are thousands of different species of frogs. Some of the most well-known species are the leopard frog, the bullfrog, and the tree frog.

Frogs have unique colors and markings.

When people think of frogs, they may imagine their bulging eyes. Or, they may picture their webbed feet and smooth, slimy-feeling skin. But, each frog species looks unique. They also live in different areas of the world.

Frogs live all over the world, except in Antarctica. They don't spend their entire life cycle in one place. They live part of their lives in water and part on land.

A Frog's Life

A frog's life cycle has three main stages. A frog begins life in an egg in the water.

When the egg hatches, the frog is born as a tadpole. A tadpole has a fishlike body with a long tail. The tadpole's body grows and changes.

In time, the tadpole grows legs. And, its tail shrinks until it becomes part of its body. Once the tadpole grows legs and no longer has a tail, it is a frog. The young frog lives on land. There, it grows into an adult. Eventually, its life ends.

Tadpoles are also called pollywogs.

Guess What?

…The only continent with no frogs is Antarctica. This is because it is too cold there!

…Some frogs have brightly patterned skin. Many of these colorful frogs are poisonous.

Brightly colored skin warns predators that a frog may be poisonous.

…The gold frog is the smallest frog species. Even as an adult, it is smaller than a dime! It measures less than one-half inch (one cm) long!

…Frogs and toads look a lot alike. How can you tell them apart? Toads have drier skin than frogs. Most toads are covered with bumpy warts, while frogs have smooth skin. And, toads have shorter legs than frogs.

Toads would rather walk than hop.

Starting To Grow

Most male frogs make croaking noises. During **mating** season, male frogs enter water and croak to attract female frogs. In this way, the females are able to find the males.

Male frogs of many species have a vocal sac that makes their call sound louder.

As the female lays eggs in the water, the male fertilizes them. The female may lay thousands of eggs at one time! This is important because many eggs will not live to be adult frogs. Inside each fertilized egg, a tadpole forms.

Tadpoles and eggs of the European common frog.

From Egg To Frog

Depending on the species, a frog egg hatches in 3 to 25 days. Then, a baby frog, or tadpole, comes out. This tadpole lives in water. And, it breathes through gills, like a fish!

Over several weeks, the tadpole gains strength. It grows back and front legs. And, it grows lungs to use instead of gills. After this happens, the tadpole is a frog. And, it can live on land. This is because it can breathe air!

This green frog still has its tail.

When this young frog first hops onto land, it still has a tail. But soon, the tail shrinks and becomes part of its body. And, the young frog grows into an adult. Some frog species go from egg to frog in 12 days. Others can take years to become frogs.

Life As An Adult

Adult frogs spend much of their lives looking for food. Frogs also spend time reproducing and working to stay alive.

Frogs are predators. They eat worms, snails, and even mice! Frogs do not chew their food. Using their sticky tongue, they catch their prey and swallow it whole. Frogs use their eyes to help them swallow their food. Their eyes sink into their skull, pushing the food down their throats.

Frogs also have to watch out for other predators. They are prey for snakes, birds, and alligators. Often, frogs can jump or hide from danger.

Egrets are one kind of bird that preys on frogs.

Endings And Beginnings

Adult frogs have different life spans. Most live between six and eight years in the wild. But, some are eaten by **predators**. Others die when their body gets old.

Poison dart frogs live in warm wet areas of South America.

Death is the end of one frog's life. But, it is not the end of the species. Because frogs can reproduce, their species continues on.

Every time a tadpole hatches from an egg, it helps create a new generation of frogs. This is the beginning of another life cycle.

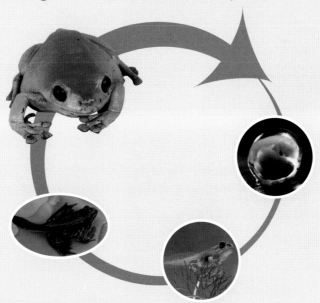

Can You Guess?

Q: How does a frog catch its prey?

A: With its fast, sticky tongue!

Q: What is the biggest frog?

A: The Goliath frog. Adults are 12 inches (30 cm) long. Some weigh as much as seven pounds (3 kg)!

Goliath frogs do not make croaking sounds. This is because they do not have a vocal sac.

Important Words

fertile able to produce seeds, fruit, or young.

generation a group that is living at the same time and is about the same age.

mate to engage in an act that leads to reproduction.

predator an animal that eats other animals.

process a way of doing something.

reproduce to produce offspring, or children.

skull the bony part of the head that protects the brain.

species living things that are very much alike.

unique different.

Web Sites

To learn more about frogs, visit ABDO Publishing Company on the World Wide Web. Web site links about frogs are featured on our Book Links page. These links are routinely monitored and updated to provide the most current information available.

www.abdopublishing.com

Index